MOLLY'S WONDROUS JOURNEY

A TOUCHING JOURNEY TO YOUR INNER SELF

MOLLY
BOOK ONE

ANNA CAMILLA KUPKA

BUTTERFLY PUBLISHING

Butterfly Publishing – Anna Camilla Kupka
Zürich, Switzerland
Text: Anna Camilla Kupka
Illustrations: Carole Isler
Editing: Ursula Tanneberger

Outside, the rain comes down in torrents. The drops drum against the windowpanes, and in the distance, thunder rolls. Molly loves this kind of weather. When it's rainy and stormy outside, and she's warm and cozy inside, time seems to slow, and she can curl up like a hedgehog without feeling guilty. Snuggled up under her blanket, she wants to read for just a few more minutes. That way, she can try to forget today when she was taunted at school again. She'd also rather not think about tomorrow, her schoolmates, and the strict teachers. Molly often finds her life exhausting. With a book, she can slip into a better, more beautiful world.

SHE MUST HAVE SOMEHOW fallen asleep because, all of a sudden, Molly finds herself in a huge laboratory swarming with activity. She looks around in amazement, her mouth wide open. All around her are tubes and vessels of every type. Everything flows, pulsates, vibrates, beats, and sways. Bits and pieces flit through the room, to be replaced by others almost as soon as they arrive. It's just like a relay race! Liquids roar through the tubing, disappearing here and there, getting sucked up and spat out once more. Tiny red and white flecks are ducking and diving. Still others divide again and again before swiftly reassembling themselves. Honeycombs form and then dissolve. Everything works in perfect harmony and time. Not one sound, not one movement, dances out of line. Molly is spellbound. What incredible, intense activity! Yet somehow, the place feels oddly familiar—as though she has always been here. She's also surprised that she's not afraid. Usually, she's not so brave. While Molly is still trying to make sense of what she sees, she hears the soft sound of a voice from within the room.

"Good evening, Molly. Welcome!"

Molly looks around but can see no one. "Where am I?" she calls out into the space.

"Well, can't you figure it out?" the voice challenges her.

"Figure it out? Of course not. I've never seen anything like this place before, not even in my wildest dreams," Molly responds, flustered, "How could I possibly figure out where I am? And who are you, anyway?"

The sound of bright laughter greets her ears. "OK, let me give you a hint. You're always right here. You can't be anywhere else. Now do you get it?"

"No, I don't." Molly is getting a bit annoyed. "So tell me already! And first, tell me who you are!"

"What you see here is your body, Molly," the voice replies, giving in. "Welcome to your own body—a true miracle! As for who I am, we'll get to that later. One thing at a time."

Molly's jaw drops. This is her body? The thousands upon thousands of processes, the bits and pieces darting about, the pumping sacks, the hustle and bustle, the whole works—all of this is inside her and exists only for her ...?

The voice can apparently read her thoughts. "Not just thousands upon thousands of processes, but millions upon millions of them, every second. Whether you're awake or asleep, feeling good or not so great, all these diligent little helpers are working around the clock—just for you."

Molly is stunned. If she tried to draw what she saw, all the pencils and paper in the world would not be enough to express it. Such harmony! She'd been to a recital of the orchestra a couple of times with her parents and always loved how the different musicians played together. But never could she have imagined that she carries an even more incredible and fascinating symphony inside, playing with no intermission or pause, just for her.

And now she notices a pumping organ that appears to be the conductor. It seems to be the control center that keeps the whole system alive. Molly watches how, with comforting regularity, it pumps red fluid into a nearly endless network of tubes.

"Is that ...?" she asks.

"Can you guess ...?" the voice replies.

Yes, this time, she can guess. This must be her heart. Mesmerized, she watches it tirelessly pumping away without a break—day in and day out. Molly feels like she's in a fairy tale. She feels big and important, like a queen. This is her kingdom! And just a few moments ago, she had no idea! Of course, she knew she had a body, but she'd never been that aware of it. And she'd certainly never experienced it quite like this before!

Molly turns fearful. She isn't dead, is she? Did she die, and now she gets to see her body one last time before forever leaving it? That wouldn't be good as she's just starting to like and be proud of it. Molly grows sad. She doesn't want to die—not yet.

The sound of friendly laughter interrupts her dark thoughts. "No, Molly, don't worry, you will not die for a long time. What's happening now is just an honorary visit inside your body. All your organs, veins, and cells are proud and grateful that you've come to see them. They feel appreciated and will now want to work even harder than before. With your visit, you spur them on —that's how happy they are to have you as their guest."

Molly is a little embarrassed. She didn't come here consciously; besides, she's only 12 years old, so should she really have so many servants? Her parents have always raised her to be modest. And now it looks like she has an entire kingdom inside her. That's a thought she'll have to get used to. But from now on, she certainly won't feel so alone anymore. After all, she always has this whole fascinating world of her body with her, which is exclusively there for her. Maybe she's not just a girl but something much, much greater ...

The thought confuses her. Molly likes to have order reign in her mind. And now she doesn't understand: if she really is inside her body, then she can't possibly be her body. You can't be inside something and be that thing at the same time. Either you're in a car, or you are the car itself. Makes sense, doesn't it? So who exactly is inside her body, anyway? Who is she?

"Good question," the voice comes to her rescue. "That's a question that has always occupied people's thoughts. And in the end, it's the only important question. That's why we're here—to find the answer."

Molly is excited. She's never pondered these sorts of

questions before. But now that they have come up, she can't wait to get the answers as soon as possible.

Once again, the voice has read her thoughts. "Don't forget, we're still at the very beginning of our journey. Try to be a little patient."

And on that note, curious and somewhat expectant, Molly follows the voice into the next room.

Earlier, while there was a never-ending bustle, it was also orderly and structured. But here, things are completely different. A vast, beautiful landscape lies before Molly, a landscape full of life and colors, cast in the richest hues. Lush green meadows, laced with shimmering golden streams, stretch as far as the eye can see. The grass sways gently in the wind, and flowers gleam in the most glorious shades. All is infinite peace, and a sleepy humming and buzzing fills the air, broken only by the bright singing of birds. The colors, joy, and ease are the loveliest thing Molly has ever seen, and she feels a deep sense of belonging and home.

The nearer she comes and the closer she looks, the more her delight grows. She can now see how the landscape came to be and how it's forever renewing itself: the streams are spun from fairies' golden hair, the air is made to dance by butterflies' fluttering wings, and the gardens are planted by brightly dressed gnomes, who seek to outdo each other in variety and vivid color.

Molly would love to run right over and play with them all, but she doesn't quite dare yet. Now, though, one by one, they start to look her way until every single one has finally turned to face her. Everyone seems glad to see her. The gnomes jump happily up and down, waving their brightly colored hats in the air. The fairies gracefully fold their hands in front of their chests and bow to her, while the butterflies dance around her head and sing her a welcoming song. Full of warmth but also a little shy, Molly returns their smiles.

With so many questions still in her head, Molly worries about looking stupid in front of the voice. But then again, she's never seen gnomes and fairies in real life before, and the voice makes no effort to explain things on its own. So soon enough, the questions just bubble up:

"Who are all these creatures? What are they doing here? And please don't ask me to figure it out again. Because I really have no idea."

Laughing, the voice comes to her aid: "These are your friends, and they're always with you. What you see before you are your feelings."

Molly looks puzzled. It's all about as clear as mud.

But the voice continues, unperturbed, "The butterflies are your playfulness and creativity, the gnomes your joy and exuberance, and the fairies your grace and your kindness."

Now Molly is really perplexed. Not that she's never thought about her feelings before, but this was certainly not how she imagined them.

The voice interrupts her musings, "You don't take a single step in life without these colorful characters right by your side. At times, one or the other will pipe up more loudly, or one will be more meddlesome than the rest. But they're always here."

Molly has to chuckle because it's true. When her feelings raise their voices, they really scramble for her attention. It can be seriously stressful sometimes, and Molly mostly tries to push them away because she has more important things to do, like meet her friends or listen to music. But now that she sees how joyful and colorful they are, she decides to pay more attention to them. She's amazed at what she's learned in the last few minutes! So not only is she the queen of a huge laboratory, her body, but apparently, she also rules over this beautiful region with its fun inhabitants. Slowly, she loses her shyness and waves excitedly at the fairies, gnomes, and butterflies.

MOLLY THEN LOOKS around some more and sees something that sends a shiver down her spine. Before her looms a huge, strangely eerie mountain. Sharp and menacing, it towers above her and seems to ward off all forms of life. Around the mountain, a slimy, disgusting river wends its way, full of ugly, croaking brown frogs that send their putrid bubbles floating to the top. This causes the sticky slime to bubble so that the river looks almost alive and even more ominous. As if to round out the picture, the river is encircled by a seemingly unbreakable, heavy iron chain. It seems insurmountable. Molly has no idea why, but the sight of it fills her with dread. Still, she has no desire to look like a coward in front of the voice, so she tries to stifle her ever-mounting panic. To distract herself, she turns back towards the beautiful landscape, yet can no longer see it out of sheer fear. Instead, her entire attention is fixed on the gray mountain and the slimy stream with the iron chain while she does her best to keep her horror at bay.

At last, she can no longer hold it in, and a loud sob escapes her lips. "You're saying all these are my feelings? The gnomes, fairies, and butterflies? And what about this slimy stream? What about this dreadful mountain and this ghastly, cold chain—what about those? Those aren't my feelings, are they?" She starts to weep uncontrollably.

The voice strokes her gently on the arm and wraps

itself around her like a warm blanket. It lets Molly cry and waits until the flood of tears has eased a bit. Then it says softly but firmly, "It's all right, dear Molly. Nothing is as bad as it looks, and nothing can happen to you. Let's move a little closer, shall we? There's something important I'd like to show you."

Before she can make up her mind, Molly notices how she's already approaching the rock. But even with the comforting presence of the voice, one cold shiver after another runs down her spine, and everything within her struggles to go on.

The voice persists, however, and encourages her some more: "Come on, Molly. You won't regret it—trust me." Hesitant, Molly keeps going.

As they get closer, Molly is amazed to realize that the landscape around the mountain is not at all as lifeless as she had thought but is bustling with activity. Crooked, sad-looking, grimy figures are carrying the heavy iron chain she saw earlier on their shoulders. Placing it around the river again and again, they make the barrier to the river and the mountain stronger and taller. They look miserable, but Molly sees no one forcing this strange behavior upon them. No overseer shouting and cracking his whip—no, the figures seem to be acting of their own accord. What a pointless situation! Molly feels boundless compassion for these hunched-over creatures and would love to free them from their burden.

At that moment, they all stop abruptly, turn in Molly's direction, and take off the chain, which at once grows thinner and thinner. The creatures sit down, wipe the sweat from their brows, and relax. Now seated in the warm sun, they all look at Molly.

As soon as the sun shines down on them, it melts away the filth that clung to them before and now flows down and off like warmed chocolate. The figures rise and stretch, and as they do so, thick scabs break off and fall from their bodies like ancient skins. Slowly they lose all stiffness and emerge as beautiful, strong, and nimble beings. Erect and alive, they blossom into the fullness of their power. Molly stares at them in awe. Not understanding the sudden change, she withdraws somewhat before this pure and powerful energy. How could something so ugly become so beautiful and majestic—and all at once?

She can make out many different figures now. First, there are wild and colorful dragons, growing bigger, brighter, and more beautiful as they spew a kaleidoscope of multicolored smoke and flame from their mouths. Their energy seems to know no bounds. Next to them, and no less impressive, are their counterparts —silent, light-gray elflike figures with beautiful, finely chiseled features. Their gentle energy is just as vital and alive as the dragons', except that it's aimed more within. Molly feels small and insignificant beside this pure life force. How stunned she is when everyone suddenly smiles and bows before her. She doesn't know what to say and looks down at the ground, slightly abashed. As she does so, her eyes fall on the iron chain, and she notices that it has meanwhile transformed into a fine, thin, and brightly gleaming silver chain. The elfin beings pick it up and place it around their necks and wrists as fine jewelry, accentuating their delicate joints. Molly feels rather plain beside such grace and shifts her gaze to the slimy river instead.

With the chain now gone, she finds nothing between herself and the stream. Her fear disappears, and she resolutely walks over to the water and looks down inside. She's astonished to see that the frogs are constantly producing the slime themselves while also struggling not to sink beneath it. They look desperate. What a sad and utterly futile endeavor. Molly shakes her head, perplexed. What is this all about? At the same time, her heart opens toward the frogs. She would love to gather them up in her arms and free them from their pain.

Right at that moment, the slime in the river begins

to disappear, and slowly the frogs relax and breathe a sigh of relief. They turn toward Molly and smile, and they, too, bow deeply before her. Molly is not as shy with the frogs as with the dragons and elves, so she bends to the frogs in turn. It seems to be the custom here. Then she watches with amazement at what happens next. The sun begins to warm the frogs, slowly causing the slime to fall away. They glow in the loveliest hues, jump high in the air for joy, kick up their heels, and croak with all their might. To Molly, their croaking no longer seems ugly but varied and full of fun. The slime is now almost completely gone, and the river turns clearer and clearer until it's so crystal clear and shining that it looks like a finely polished mirror.

Molly can hardly tear her eyes away. These wondrous changes have left her utterly spellbound. Then bit by bit, she feels herself growing anxious again. There's still one thing she must dare to face: the mountain! While the landscape around it has transformed into a gloriously colored scene, bathed in all manner of hues from the dragon's brilliant fire, the mountain looms unchanged above it all, sheer and cold. Yet, like magic, it draws Molly nearer. She slowly ventures toward it—something she wouldn't have dreamed of just a few minutes ago! As she approaches the mountain, she doesn't see any living creatures this time but instead hears noises from within. It seems to be hollow inside, much like a volcano. Hesitant, Molly stops in her tracks.

"Come on," urges the voice. "Let's look inside."

Now Molly is truly glad that the voice is still with her. After all, she hasn't regained her confidence quite that much. Together, Molly and the voice climb up the mountain, which no longer seems so big to her. Once at the top, she summons up all her courage and looks inside. What she sees there almost breaks her heart: a small, haggard creature is digging rocks out of the ground and building the mountain around itself—higher and higher and narrower and narrower. It's shutting itself off from the world outside while building a wall around itself. It's a heartrending, terrifying task. Molly feels a terrible chill.

"What did this small, innocent creature do to punish itself so much?" she asks the voice.

At that moment, the figure looks up, and the sunlight falls upon its little face and wide eyes. Molly instinctively reaches down into the mountain and slowly lifts it out. The mountain immediately collapses upon itself and vanishes into the ground. In its place, flowers sprout from the earth all around Molly's feet. Still terrified, the figure curls up in Molly's hand, its whole body shaking. It's too afraid to look at the light and tries to make itself as small as possible. Molly gently presses the little form against herself to warm and soothe it. Then she lifts it up and breathes a kiss on its forehead. Slowly, the figure raises its head and looks right into Molly's eyes. It seems to Molly that they've known each other forever, so deep is the bond she feels between them.

"Who are you?" Molly asks softly.

But though the figure has grown somewhat calmer, it still trembles like a leaf and stares at her in silence.

"This figure embodies your fear," the voice quietly chimes in.

"My fear?" Molly replies in a hoarse tone, astonished. "But why does it build this mountain around itself? That doesn't make any sense! It will just suffer even more!" And once again, the tears stream down her cheeks.

"You know, most people would rather not face their fear but try to push it away instead," the voice replies softly. "Which is why fear hides and builds a higher and higher mountain around itself. But it is nothing to be afraid of. You're much bigger than your fear."

And it's true. Molly is indeed much bigger than her fear. Fear doesn't seem to be something you need to hide from, after all, or something you need to force into hiding. It looks so tiny and helpless in her hand. Molly feels deep compassion.

"And who are these?" she asks, pointing at the frogs. "And these? ... and these?" She looks at the dragons and the elflike beings.

"Come on. Let's go over and see," says the voice.

With her fear safely tucked in her hand, Molly and the voice walk over to the place where all the freed beings now sit together in the sun. She gently lets her fear slide to the ground, where it immediately makes itself comfortable among the others, who take it protectively into their midst. It seems that here it feels safe and sound. Little by little, it starts to relax. Less shaky and tense, it begins to radiate peace and calm. Molly feels a deep love for it and is relieved that she was able to help. She has the feeling that her heart keeps growing bigger and bigger.

That's when she hears the voice again, anticipating her next question: "You wanted to know who the frogs were, didn't you? These frogs, Molly, embody your sense of shame that always arises when you feel embarrassed by something."

An image immediately pops into Molly's head of

when she came out of the restroom at school with her dress still tucked in her underwear. The laughter was unbearable. She still blushes just thinking about it. She would rather forget about it right away and suppress her shame. But then it occurs to her that all these creatures here were released the moment she took them into her heart and showed them compassion. Is that what the voice wants her to see? She deliberately looks back on that painful moment at school and immediately feels ashamed again. But she notices that it no longer matters so much to her and that she can calmly let the feeling be. It is, after all, a totally normal feeling. Shame belongs to this colorful landscape as much as anything else. Molly feels somehow liberated.

But now she's curious. She wants to find out what the dragons and the noble elfin beings are. Maybe the dragons are her anger? To test it, she thinks of her little brother and how he likes to tease her. Instantly, the dragons spit more fire. It's almost fun to let the anger come out like this and to feel its heat. Molly decides to play with her rage some more. She sees that it can help her express herself, to blow off some real steam. Another freeing and powerful feeling! She is full of energy, and it's almost as if she were flying over the countryside on a dragon's back.

Now she wonders who the noble elfin beings are,
the ones who so intimidate her with their beauty. She
senses a deep connection with them and feels that
they're close to her heart. But no matter how hard she
tries to think of it, she has no idea what they could be.

The voice comes to her help: "These beautiful
beings are a part of you as well. They are your grief."

Without warning, the image of Molly's dead
grandma appears before her mind's eye, and she feels a
painful stab in her chest. She knows the feeling of grief
all too well. But she never saw it as beautiful—quite
the opposite. Once more, the tears well up in her eyes.

"Molly, allow your tears to flow," the voice consoles
her. "Respect your grief, which is born of love for your
grandma. Grief has an infinite grace and wants to be
appreciated in all its deep and tender beauty. When

you can look your feelings in the eye, see their worth, their beauty, and fragility, too ... and finally, when you can lovingly embrace them, they turn into something beautiful. But when you push them away, they also deny themselves. It's then that you feel the mountain built by the fear that you suppress. You sense it in your stomach in the morning before you go to school. When your anger is stifled, instead of letting off steam, it wraps itself around your neck like a chain, depriving you of the air you need to breathe. Equally, your tears of sadness want to flow. But these, too, are suppressed. And since grief often goes hand in hand with anger over something you've lost, they forge the chain together to hold themselves in check. But you see now that as soon as you accept your feelings as they are, everything transforms into new life. Love changes all."

Molly thinks it over. "Yeah, it's kind of easy here," she finally answers. "But right now, I'm in the middle of a dream or something. Normally though, I can't see my feelings, and they often hurt so much. And besides, you're here with me now. Mostly, I'm alone, and there's no way I can do this by myself."

"You can always see your feelings, Molly, if you take the time to travel inside yourself. Just close your eyes and sense what's within. Feelings can't cause pain. It's the suppression of your feelings that causes the pain. Feelings can be big and strong and powerful, but that's this colorful life—it's all part of it. Suppressing life, that's what causes the pain. Feelings can never harm you. They're energies that want to dance and play, but they're never dangerous."

Molly nods. She's beginning to understand. Laughter and tears, sorrow and joy—they're all just part of what makes up her vibrant emotional land-scape. Molly has the impression that everything might be easier than she thought. Maybe she'll be able to pay more attention to her feelings from now on. At least, she can try.

"All right, let's go a little higher," the voice says. "You don't need to say goodbye to your new friends—they're always here with you. But now I'd like you to meet some more of your allies."

And with that, Molly and the voice find themselves in an infinite expanse. This is how Molly had always imagined the universe. Everything is bright blue and crystal clear. Flashes of the most beautiful and brilliant colors pass through space like exploding firecrackers, taking on a variety of shapes and then disappearing again. It's just like the fireworks display she once saw with her parents, where she couldn't tear her eyes away. The lightning flashes shine with unimaginable power and clarity and have an energy that makes the air vibrate. Molly watches in delight and finally asks the voice what this is.

"These are your thoughts!"

"My thoughts?," Molly repeats. She's gradually reaching the point where nothing surprises her anymore. "How so?"

"Let's do a little experiment," the voice prompts her. "Think of something you love."

Molly loves to sing, and the very second she thinks of it, the fireworks become even grander and more colorful and brilliant.

"And now imagine yourself on stage as a famous singer, delighting the hearts of your audience."

Molly clearly sees the picture in front of her, and the fireworks explode in colors she's never seen before. Wow! She really did that herself? Molly's face beams.

She goes on and on, imagining the craziest things. What fun!!

Her imagination knows no bounds, and she comes up with more and more amazing ideas. The fireworks make the whole sky glow. Her mind is like an endless treasure chest—she can conjure up anything she wants. Molly jumps around with joy. The voice cheers her on, laughing, encouraging her to create her very own multicolored realm. Everything is allowed, no matter what.

"Wow, this is awesome," Molly whoops. She's rarely had this much fun. But then, in one part of the heavenly vault, she makes out a couple of dark clouds that stand in the way of her fireworks' brilliant colors, and she asks the voice where they come from.

"The clouds are created by your negative thoughts."

"What do you mean by negative thoughts?" Molly asks.

"Well, any thoughts that aren't good for you."

"What's that supposed to mean?"

"Think about it: what thought doesn't feel good? Can you think of one?"

Molly considers this. Finally, something occurs to her. "My father always says: 'There's no such thing as a free lunch.' He means that nothing is given without a price. That doesn't feel good. And it sounds very expensive!"

The voice laughs. "Very expensive indeed! But is this thought true?"

Molly thinks again. "Well, sort of." Then she hesitates. "Although, I'm no longer so sure about that. Suddenly, I discovered a whole exciting lab inside myself. I've found a new set of friends in my feelings, and now I've also realized that I can create fireworks with my thoughts. And I didn't even do anything to make it all happen. You could see that as a gift, couldn't you?"

The voice smiles (a voice can smile, too—Molly knows that now). "You've understood it well."

But before the voice can go on, Molly eagerly interrupts: "That reminds me, I can get a lot more in my mind than I can in the world outside. I just have to think of it, and there it is. For example: airplanes must first be built, then a ticket costs a lot of money, and you have to fly a long time to get to a faraway place. But in my imagination, I can travel to a desert in Africa in one split second, and from there to the rainforests in Australia ... and then to the moon if I want to. I just have to imagine it, and poof—I'm in the middle of it! If I want, I can see tigers and lions in front of me, paint them brightly in my mind and make them tame or leave them wild. Because you know what? I have the whole universe inside me in every possible way, shape, and form. I just have to imagine something, and there it is. It's that easy. That's a gift!" Molly is so excited she's tripping over her words.

"That's exactly right," the voice replies cheerfully. "Your inner life is infinitely rich, and you may enjoy this richness every day anew and experiment with your thoughts as much as you like. But always check your thoughts to see if they feel good. Only then are they really colorful and alive. It's a never-ending game, and you'll have lots of fun being creative. Everything people have created so far has started in their imagination. But now it's time to bring you to the most wonderful place of all."

With these words, a magnificent golden gate appears, adorned with delicate ornaments and reaching all the way up to the sky. Molly suddenly feels small again and shies away from this splendor.

"Be brave. Go right on through—that's why we're here!" The voice encourages her and gives her a gentle nudge.

"And what about you?" Molly asks in a slight panic. "Aren't you coming?"

"This part you can do alone. I'll wait for you here," the voice replies.

Molly takes a deep breath, closes her eyes for a moment, gathers her courage, and walks through the gate.

Now on the other side, Molly feels herself enfolded by the blissful warmth of a thousand loving arms. All forms and colors dissolve. Never has she felt such oneness before. Infinite comfort and assurance surround her on all sides and flow throughout her being. All is simply right. All is perfect—bright and pure, like the radiance of the world's most pristine, softest light. It has no color, yet it holds all colors within itself. There also reigns a stillness so complete that it embraces all the music in the world and, at the same time, is the source of it all. And Molly feels that she's a part of it, that she belongs here. The silence speaks to her. But the way she hears the silence is different from the way she listened to the voice before. She doesn't hear it with her ears. Instead, the words well up from deep within as a soft song that gently sways through every fiber of her being.

"Welcome, Molly."

"Thank you," Molly responds and quietly asks: "Where am I?"

"You're now in your innermost being, your true nature. After passing through your body, then taking on the challenges of your emotional landscape and getting to know the universe of your thoughts, you've now returned to your innermost being—to Love." The response comes as tender as a caress.

"To Love?" Molly repeats, amazed.

"Yes, to Love."

Molly hesitates slightly. "And who are you?"

"I am the voice of your heart. And your heart is a trusted messenger of Love."

"And what exactly is Love?" Molly asks.

"Love is the source of all," the voice replies in a whisper.

"The source of all?"

"Yes."

Molly ponders briefly.

"And what does that mean: the source of all?"

"Everything comes from Love and returns to Love. Love, on the other hand, is eternal. Your body is a creation of Love: it comes from Love and returns to it again. Your feelings are a creation of Love: they, too, come from Love and return to it again. The same is true of your thoughts. But you, in your innermost being—you are Love, and Love never ceases!"

Molly has to digest this for a moment.

Finally, she asks, "Is Love the source of bad things, too?"

"They also come from Love. They are a child that was born of Love but has closed its heart for a moment. That's why it can't hear my voice. Yet, Love also loves this child."

"But if Love also loves bad things, then will anything ever change on this earth?"

"Yes. Because more and more people are opening themselves to the voice of the heart and, just as you did now, are becoming aware of Love as their true nature. Once you become aware that your innermost being is infinite Love, you no longer want to do anything bad."

"Why not?"

"Because when you see that everything comes from the same source and that your innermost being can never be harmed, you live in harmony with yourself and the world. Then there is nothing more to fight and nothing to defend."

These words have an instant effect on Molly. Inside, she begins to open and expand. She allows the voice of her heart to have more and more room, to wholly fill her being. A vast sense of peace unfolds within her, and she feels a profound change taking place inside. She releases a deep sigh, and a smile of relief settles on her face. How beautiful this is!

"AND WHO WAS the voice that walked with me before?" she quietly asks. "Was that you, too?"

"That voice also belongs to a messenger of Love. It's the voice of an angel—your own guardian angel, dear Molly. The one who constantly watches over you and whose wings hover above you like a shield."

And with that, Molly falls into a deep sleep once more, and her guardian angel carries her back to bed. But nothing will be the same again. For now, she knows how to treasure her body. She's learned to embrace her feelings and to play and experiment with her thoughts. And should she ever feel lost and confused, she only needs to ask: "What would Love do?" And her heart will know the answer.

DID YOU LIKE THE STORY?

We sincerely hope you enjoyed MOLLY'S WONDROUS JOURNEY! If you liked the story, you will also cherish the sequels:

MOLLY ENCHANTS HER WORLD
MOLLY BOOK 2

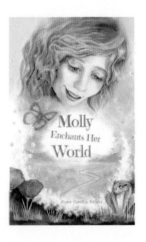

After Molly's wondrous journey to her inner world, she wonders what it's like inside other people. Do they feel and think the same as she does, or is everyone really different? And once again, Molly finds herself on an adventure that not only answers that question but, to her amazement, also shows her how to transform and truly enchant the world around her.

MOLLY, ARCHITECT OF LIFE
MOLLY BOOK 3

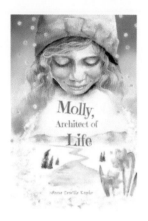

After her extraordinary journeys, Molly now knows about her inner life and the inner lives of others. But she wouldn't be Molly if a new question wasn't gnawing at her: is her guardian angel right when he claims she can create exactly the life she wants? And is it really as easy as child's play? Molly has her doubts, but she sets out to find out!

ABOUT THE AUTHOR

Anna Camilla Kupka grew up in Düsseldorf/Germany, where she first studied law and then earned her doctorate at the University of Münster. She subsequently attended the Stanford Graduate School of Business in California/USA and lived in Dublin/Ireland for a long time. Today, Anna lives and loves in Zurich/Switzerland. She believes that happiness is our birthright, and she is especially committed to helping young people recognize and live their full potential.

Printed in Great Britain
by Amazon

19129680R00025